THREAT TO THE BENGAL TIGER

Claire O'Neal

P.O. Box 196
Hockessin, Delaware 19707
Visit us on the web: www.mitchelllane.com
Comments? email us: mitchelllane@mitchelllane.com

Printing   1   2   3   4   5   6   7   8   9

A Robbie Reader/On the Verge of Extinction: Crisis in the Environment

Library of Congress Cataloging-in-Publication Data
O'Neal, Claire.
  Threat to the Bengal tiger / by Claire O'Neal.
      p. cm. — (On the verge of extinction. Crisis in the environment)
  "A Robbie Reader."
  Includes bibliographical references and index.
  ISBN 978-1-58415-688-8 (library bound : alk. paper)
  1. Tigers—Juvenile literature. 2. Endangered species—Juvenile literature. 3. Tigers—Conservation—Juvenile literature. I. Title.
  QL737.C23O59 2009
  333.95'97560954—dc22
                                                    2008020891

ABOUT THE AUTHOR: Dr. Claire O'Neal first learned about tigers when she visited the zoo as a child. She was fascinated that such big, dangerous animals played together just like humans do. Since then, she attended Indiana University and the University of Washington, earning degrees in English, biology, and chemistry. She has written articles for scientific publications, poetry, and books for children including *How to Convince Your Parents You Can Care for a Pet Horse* for Mitchell Lane Publishers. She lives in Delaware and enjoys taking her own children to visit the zoo and watch the tigers.

PHOTO CREDITS: Cover, background photos, pp. 1, 8, 11, 13, 19, 21, 25—JupiterImages; p. 4—Monique Hofland; p. 7—AP Photo/Brian Cassey; p. 12—Seaworld.org; p. 14—AP Photo/File; p. 15—Mila Zinkova/ CC-BY-SA-2.5; p. 16—SavetheTigerFund.org; p. 18—Againess/ CC-SA-2.5; p. 22—AP Photo/Dita Alangkara; p. 24—Indian Dance Research Center N.G.O; p. 27—SaveChinasTigers.org; p. 28—AP Photo/K. M. Chaudary.

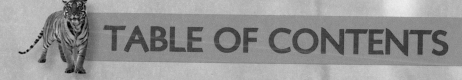

TABLE OF CONTENTS

Words in **bold** type can be found in the glossary.

EXTINCTION

A tiger's paws are important in many ways. Claws lie within them, retracted (pulled in) until a tiger stretches out its paw to kill. Between the claws are scent glands. When tigers scratch themselves, trees, or prey, they leave behind smelly information for other tigers. Tiger paws also leave tracks called pug marks. Pug marks are the main way tiger researchers keep track of tigers.

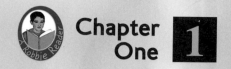

THE TIGER AND THE MOUSE

The power and intelligence of tigers gives them an important place in the culture, imagination, and **mythology** of the people of Southeast Asia, as shown by this folktale from Cambodia:

A tiger wandered to a pond in the scorching jungle heat. A thirsty mouse was drinking there already. The tiger licked its lips and crept noiselessly toward this potential snack. With a quick swipe, the mouse was trapped in the tiger's paws.

"Mouse, you are so puny," said the hungry tiger, "but I think I'll eat you anyway."

The mouse struggled and squirmed in vain against the tiger's grasp. He squeaked at the tiger, pleading for his life. "Please, sir, let me go! I am very small, I admit. I certainly wouldn't make much of a meal for you. But you never know, sir, when a friend like me may come in handy."

The tiger nearly collapsed from laughter. A mouse as his friend? It was too much. Wiping tears from his eyes, he set the mouse free. "I can't imagine when I would need a friend like you, Mouse. But you are bold, I'll give you that. I will spare your life today. Besides, if I ate you, I would still be hungry."

The next day the tiger roamed the jungle looking for something to eat. Suddenly, he was lifted off the ground and was hanging upside down in a net of rope. He had sprung a trap made by hunters from the village. He struggled and squirmed but could not free himself from the thick cords.

Before long, the mouse walked by and looked up at the helpless tiger. "Oh my, Tiger," he said, "what has happened to you?"

"Please, friend Mouse, can you help me? I am caught in a trap. If the hunters find me,

A tiger's roar contains many different sounds made all at once, some too low to be heard by human ears. These low sounds can travel up to two miles.

they will surely kill me!" The mouse quickly remembered the tiger's kindness from before. He jumped onto the net and chewed through the ropes with his sharp teeth. In no time the trap came crashing to the ground, freeing the tiger. The tiger could not thank him enough, and told him that he would remember his kindness forever.

Just as in this ancient story, the tiger doesn't stand a chance against humans, its only natural enemy. Tigers are threatened with **extinction** (ek-STINK-shun). Does the tiger have any friends left to save it today?

EXTINCTION

Tigers hunt at dusk and dawn, when their stripes help them hide in the long shadows. The pattern of a tiger's stripes is unique; no two tigers are alike. Chinese culture reveres the tiger partly because the marks on a tiger's forehead look like the Chinese character wang, meaning "king."

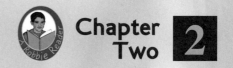

IT'S HARD AT THE TOP

Tigers are classified into six different **subspecies**, or types, based on where they live. The Bengal tiger is the most famous and most numerous. It can be found in China, Bhutan, Nepal, and Myanmar, but most of them live in India and Bangladesh, in an area that used to be called Bengal.

Tigers (species name *Panthera tigris*) are the largest land-living, meat-eating animal on the planet. They grow to be 10 feet long from head to tail and can weigh 500 pounds. They have a fiery orange coat with dark stripes that **camouflages** (KAA-muh-flah-jes) them against forest shadows or tall grasses. Tigers have adapted to an amazing variety of habitats in Southeast Asia—grasslands, evergreen forests, rain forests, and even swamps. All they need to survive is shade in which to hide, water to drink, and a steady source of prey.

The life of a Bengal tiger is dangerous from the start. Tiger cubs are born completely helpless and depend on their mother for everything. Many die at birth from disease or starvation. A tigress cares for her cubs until they are two to three years old. She protects them from other **predators** (PREH-duh-terz), including male tigers, and teaches them how to hunt and kill.

To survive, a young adult must find its own territory, a large piece of land in which it can sleep and hunt. All tigers are **solitary** (SAH-lih-tayr-ee) animals that fiercely protect their territories. They mark their boundaries with strong scents that tell other tigers to stay away. To gain a territory, a young tiger may fight to take over the territory of another tiger. The first owner is probably older and more experienced, and it may fight to the

Male tigers sometimes enter bloody or even deadly battles over territories. These territories contain both food and females—things worth dying for if you are a male tiger.

death to keep its home. The young tiger may also move into an empty territory at the edge of the habitat, near villages. Without much prey in this area, tigers may hunt **livestock**. Farmers get angry when tigers eat their animals, and they will ask the government to hunt the tiger down. A lucky tiger in the wild might live to its eighteenth birthday.

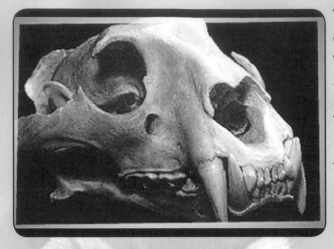

The canine teeth of adult male tigers can be 3 inches long, the biggest of any cat. These teeth are loaded with nerves that help a tiger sense the hard and soft parts of prey as it bites down.

Once it gains a territory, new challenges face the tiger. Tigers prey on mainly deer and antelope, which can easily outrun them. Tigers also hunt bigger animals, such as cattle, buffalo, wild pigs, and even young

A Bengal tiger eats its latest kill, a deer. After the tiger leaves, a whole ecosystem of scavengers—mammals, birds, reptiles, and even insects—will eat, too.

elephants. These animals are strong and have hooves and horns, tusks, or antlers that they use for defense. The tiger is very cautious to avoid getting hurt. Only one out of every 10 or 20 hunts ends in a kill. A tiger's life is full of peril, but historically, this has kept tiger populations in check. If there were too many tigers in an area, there would not be enough food to go around.

Unlike their housecat cousins, tigers love to swim. They will even swim to chase prey. This tiger is cooling off in the river on a hot day.

Tigers can run fast for short distances, but many animals they hunt are too speedy to chase down. Instead, tigers hunt by surprise attack, quietly moving close before pouncing.

On average, tigers kill about once a week. They gorge themselves on fresh meat—a tiger can eat up to 80 pounds in one sitting. Just to stay alive, an adult male tiger needs to eat almost 8,000 pounds of meat in a year. This means a tiger is always hunting.

EXTINCTION

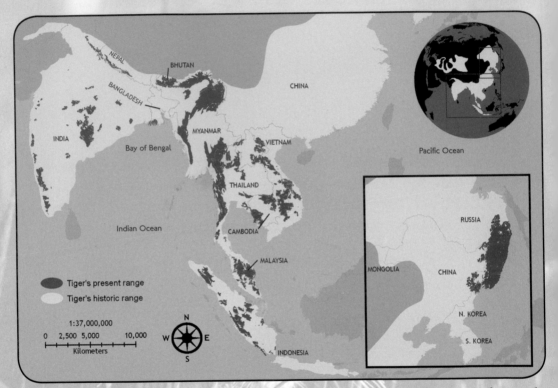

Wild tigers used to number in the hundreds of thousands and roam through parts of Europe and much of Asia (yellow). Now their territory is split up (green), and their numbers are so low that all six subspecies of tiger are considered endangered. The Bengal tiger is from an area that used to be called Bengal. That area is in present-day Bangladesh and northeastern India.

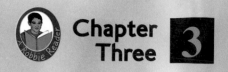
THREATS TO THE BENGAL TIGER

In the early 1900s, Indian officials estimated that 40,000 Bengal tigers lived in the wild. By 1972, the Bengal tiger population had shrunk to only 1,500. Wild tigers are vanishing, and researchers believe that people are to blame.

Worldwide, selling tiger body parts is against the law. But laws do not always stop people from stealing a piece of tiger magic for themselves. Tiger skins and heads are prized for clothing and decorations. People who practice ancient Chinese medicine falsely believe that tiger bones can help heal **arthritis** (ar-THRY-tus) in humans. To meet the growing demand, illegal hunters called **poachers** kill many wild tigers every year.

Because of stricter laws and falling tiger numbers, fewer tigers are illegally killed today than ever before. However, dead tigers are worth a lot of money on the black market. A whole tiger carcass can bring $160,000 to poachers in Southeast Asia.

Poaching is dangerous. Hunters risk going to jail or getting hurt or killed themselves by wild animals—or even by other poachers. However, poaching continues because some people will pay a lot for a dead tiger. The pelt can sell for $10,000 on the **black market**.

Poaching laws can be difficult to enforce. In India, for example, park rangers do not carry guns. They cannot stop heavily armed poachers. More tigers die each year from being shot or poisoned than from natural causes.

Perhaps the greatest threat to the tiger is the loss of its natural habitat. Tigers once roamed through all of Southeast Asia. Now, the human populations of these countries are growing faster than anywhere else on Earth.

The Bengal tiger loses more of its habitat every day to human development. Today, tigers like this one have a better chance at survival in zoos than in the wild.

This tiger lives in a reserve. Although poaching is still a danger in reserves, these areas may be the last hope for the wild tiger.

More and more people are moving to areas where tigers are wild, simply because there is no room anywhere else. They cut down forests or fill in swamps where tigers live to build new homes, businesses, or roads. It is doubtful the tiger will ever get this land back.

Tigers will not cross human-occupied land, so they are trapped inside protected national parks or tiger reserves. The land occupied by tigers in 2008 made up less than 7 percent of their historical range.

Older tiger cubs wrestle after a swim. Tiger cubs play with each other to practice skills they will need to hunt and fight as adults.

Tigers suffer when they are restricted this way. If enough of certain plants or water sources are destroyed, prey populations may decrease, and tigers could run out of food. Because they are **isolated** (Y-soh-lay-ted) in small communities, related tigers may breed, which produces sickly cubs. When this happens, tiger populations have less of a chance of survival.

EXTINCTION

A three-month old Bengal tiger cub is fed milk by its keeper in a zoo in Indonesia. In the wild, cubs drink only their mother's milk for up to two months. They will stay with her, learning how to hunt, for two years.

IS THERE HOPE?

The future for wild Bengal tigers does not look good, but tigers in India probably have the best chance of survival. Since 1973, the Indian government has run Project Tiger, a **conservation** (kon-ser-VAY-shun) effort to manage national parks and other protected areas where tigers live.

By 2008, India had 40 protected tiger homes. Unfortunately, those reserves may not stay protected forever. New laws in India may allow people to claim the protected land as their own, if their ancestors belonged to native tribes. If the government loses interest in the reserves, the land could easily be used for mines, roads, farms, and power plants to serve the growing population.

The tiger's biggest problem is that its human neighbors are desperately poor. The average person in India earns only about $1,000 per year. People living near tiger reserves, away from cities, earn much less. (By comparison, the average person in the United States makes $35,000 per year.) In tiger countries, it can be difficult to care about the plight of the tiger when people can't afford to live. When a tiger's land is given to developers, it brings jobs and money to that area. Poaching tigers puts food on the table for the hunter's family. As tiger authority John

Children work at their jobs in a brickyard. Many families in rural India are so poor that they will starve unless their children go to work.

Seidensticker says, "Tigers won't ultimately be safe until they're worth more alive than dead."

To help tigers earn their keep, many national parks in India use tigers as a tourist attraction. When people from all over the world come to see the tigers, they stay in local villages and spend money there. When a local villager has a job as a tour guide, he or she is encouraged to protect the tiger and educate travelers about the tiger, its beauty, and its struggles.

Rarely, tigers are born with white fur, like these white Bengal tigers. They are not albino because they have dark stripes and blue eyes. (Albino animals are all white with red eyes.) In Korea, paintings of the white tiger are kept in homes to ward off evil.

Li Quan (in pink), founder of the Save China's Tigers Foundation, stands with a banner signed by 10,000 tiger supporters. The South China tiger may be closer to extinction than the Bengal tiger subspecies.

Many experts agree that tigers will be around in zoos for generations to come. Tigers in zoos breed well. In 2008, captive tigers outnumbered wild tigers four to one! They also outlive wild tigers by almost 10 years. But unless people act to save the tigers' land, tigers will certainly go extinct in the wild.

A mother and her cubs are protected in a zoo in China. Tigers are important to the traditions of Southeast Asia. In Hindu myth from India, the goddess Parvati rides on a tiger. The powerful god Shiva wears a tiger skin. The Chinese calendar celebrates a Year of the Tiger. In each culture, tigers are considered intelligent and powerful.

If the wild tiger goes extinct, its human neighbors will lose an important cultural figure. Indian leader Mahatma Gandhi once said, "The greatness of a nation and its moral progress can be judged by the way its animals are treated." How can we judge what the world has lost if we take the wild out of the tiger?

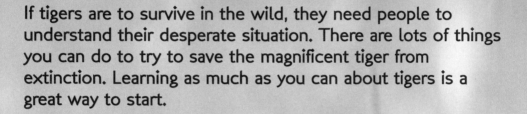

If tigers are to survive in the wild, they need people to understand their desperate situation. There are lots of things you can do to try to save the magnificent tiger from extinction. Learning as much as you can about tigers is a great way to start.

- Read books on tigers from your library, or check out conservation web sites online.
- Visit tigers at your local zoo. Find out what your zoo is doing to help tigers around the world.
- Encourage your school to do a research project on tigers.

The research and conservation efforts that are keeping tigers in the wild need your help, too. Organizations such as the World Wildlife Fund (http://www.wwf.org) and Save the Tiger Fund (http://www.savethetigerfund.org) work with scientists and governments to save tigers. These organizations need a lot of money to do their jobs well. Can you find ways to raise money to help tigers?

- You can donate your own money. Every little bit helps. Or you could ask your parents or relatives to make a donation to tiger research.
- Host a lemonade stand, a bake sale, or a yard sale. Advertise that the profits will help save the tigers. Donate the money you earn.
- For your next birthday party, ask people to donate to tiger research instead of spending their money on presents for you.

Books

Kipling, Rudyard. *The Jungle Book.* New York: Dover Publications, 2000.

Montgomery, Sy. *Man-Eating Tigers of the Sundarbans.* New York: Houghton Mifflin, 2001.

Spilsbury, Richard A., and Louise A. Spilsbury. *Bengal Tiger.* Portsmouth, New Hampshire: Heinemann, 2006.

Swain, Gwenyth. *Tigers.* Minnetonka, Minnesota: T&N Children's Publishing, 2002.

Works Consulted

Bly, Laura. "Tigers' Fate Is Still Uncertain." *USA Today,* November 29, 2007.

Corbett, Jim. *Man-Eaters of Kumaon.* New York: Oxford University Press, 1946.

Ellis, Richard. *Tiger Bone & Rhino Horn.* Washington, D.C.: Island Press, 2005.

Ives, Richard. *Of Tigers & Men: Entering the Age of Extinction.* New York: Doubleday, 1996.

Karanth, K. Ullas. *The Way of the Tiger.* Stillwater, Minnesota: Voyageur Press, 2001.

Mazák, Vratislav. "*Panthera tigris.*" MAMMALIAN SPECIES NO. 152, pp. 1–8, 3 figs. Published May 8, 1981, by The American Society of Mammalogists. http://www. science.smith.edu/departments/ Biology/VHAYSSEN/msi/pdf/152_ Panthera_tigris.pdf

McCarthy, Susan. *Becoming a Tiger.* New York: HarperCollins Publishers, 2004.

Meacham, Cory J. *How the Tiger Lost Its Stripes.* New York: Harcourt Brace & Company, 1997.

O'Connor, Anahad. "The Story and the Tiger." *New York Times,* December 26, 2007.

Riding the Tiger. Eds. John Seidensticker, Sarah Christie, and Peter Jackson. Cambridge, UK: Cambridge University Press, 1999.

Sankhala, Kailash. *Tiger!* New York: Simon and Schuster, 1977.

Sunquist, Fiona, and Mel Sunquist. *Tiger Moon.* Chicago: The University of Chicago Press, 1988.

Thapar, Valmik. *Tigers.* Emmaus, Pennsylvania: Rodale Press, 1989.

On the Internet

Cyber Tiger at National Geographic http://www.nationalgeographic. com/tigers/maina.html?fs=animals- panther.nationalgeographic.com

Geoguide: Tiger. "Eyes on the Tiger" http://www.nationalgeographic. com/education/geoguide/tigers/ index.html

Save the Tiger Fund http://www.savethetigerfund.org/

Tiger Care at the Bronx Zoo http://savingtigers.com/st-home/ st-bztigercare

World Wildlife Fund Tiger Page http://www.worldwildlife.org/ tigers/

arthritis (ar-THRY-tus)—Pain or swelling in the joints.

black market—The trade of illegal goods.

camouflage (KAA-muh-flahj)—Body coloring that helps an animal hide in its habitat.

conservation (kon-ser-VAY-shun)—Preserving animals, plants, or land, usually with government help.

ecosystem (EE-koh-sis-tum)—The community of plants and animals in an area.

endangered (en-DAYN-jerd)—Almost extinct; when relatively few individuals of a species are alive.

extinction (ek-STINK-shun)—When no more individuals of a species are alive.

isolated (Y-soh-lay-ted)—Alone; separated from others.

livestock (LYV-stok)—Animals farmed for profit.

mythology (mih-THAH-luh-jee)—Stories and beliefs of a culture that help explain their world.

poacher (POH-chur)—One who hunts illegally.

predators (PREH-duh-terz)—Animals that hunt other animals for food.

reveres (ree-VEERS)—Honors and respects.

solitary (SAH-lih-tayr-ee)—Alone; by itself.

subspecies (SUB-spee-sheez)—A large, identifiable group of individuals within a species, usually separated from others of its species by its location.

INDEX